Also by Steve Goodier

Riches of the Heart
Joy Along the Way
Prescription for Peace
Touching Moments

Please see the **Quick** **Order** **Form** at the
back of this book.

One Minute Can Change a Life

Sixty-Second Readings of Hope and Encouragement

Steve Goodier

Second Edition

Life Support System♡Publishing, Inc.
P.O. Box 237 Divide, CO 80814
www.LifeSupportSystem.com

One Minute Can Change a Life

Sixty-Second Readings of Hope and Encouragement

By Steve Goodier

Life Support System♡ Publishing, Inc.
P.O. Box 237 Divide, CO 80814

Library of Congress Card Number: 99-091224

ISBN 1-929664-00-1 (Soft cover)

Cover design: Brent Stewart

Contents

Your Support System

Have you noticed how help is often available just when you need it? A few years ago, a California artist carved a unique Christmas gift for his parents in Connecticut. It was a four-foot-tall statue of a hitchhiker, with thumb extended. (The perfect gift for the discriminating homeowner...) His gift was unusual, but his method of shipping the statue to his folks was even stranger. He simply set it beside the road and let it "hitch" its way across the continent. Around the statue's neck he hung a sign bearing his parents' New England address, and across its chest was printed the word "Connecticut" in large letters. Several weeks and some 2,500 miles later, unknown hands delivered the gift to the woodcarver's parents in time for Christmas.

I find it heartening to remember that there are always those willing to help. And it's true regardless of the circumstance. There is someone willing to extend a hand, lend an ear or share a heart. Whether you need temporary assistance or your life has experienced a meltdown, there is someone who wants to help.

In every important way, you are never really alone. You have a life "support system" consisting of people you may have never met! And it's one of your greatest resources.

Stick To It

According to William S. Banowsky, the story of one of America's greatest leaders is actually a story of repeated failures and dogged persistence:

In 1831 he failed in business.
In 1832 he was defeated for the state legislature.
In 1833 he failed again in business.
In 1834 he was elected to the state legislature.
In 1835 his sweetheart died.
In 1836 he had a nervous breakdown.
In 1838 he was defeated for Speaker.
In 1840 he was defeated for Elector.
In 1843 he was defeated for Congress.
In 1846 he was elected for one term to Congress.
In 1848 he was defeated again for Congress.
In 1855 he was defeated for the Senate.
In 1856 he was defeated for Vice President.
In 1858 he was defeated again for the Senate.

In 1860 he, finally, was elected President of the United States. And these are just a few of the rough spots in the life of Abraham Lincoln.

Someone said, "Failure is the line of least persistence." My mother called it "stick-to-it- iv-ness." It generally boils down to a healthy combination of faith and hard work, and it usually means success.

Are you feeling discouraged? Perhaps you just need to give it one more try.

P.S.

Some advice Abe Lincoln didn't follow: If at first you don't succeed, blame someone else and seek counseling....

Won't Power

A certain man was on a diet to lose weight. He even changed routes to work in order to avoid a particular bakery, which displayed scrumptious looking pastries in its window. But one day he arrived at the office carrying a beautiful, large coffee cake. His colleagues teased him about slipping off the diet.

In reply, he smiled and said, "Today I *accidentally* drove by the bakery and looked in the window and saw a host of goodies. Now, I felt it was no accident, so I prayed, 'Lord, if you want me to have one of these delicious coffee cakes, let me find a parking space in front of the bakery.' And sure enough, the eighth time around the block, *there it was!*"

Sometimes "will power" is simply "won't power." It's about finding the inner power to say, "I *won't* continue in this behavior or attitude."

Self-discipline is an essential part of building a whole and healthy life. Do you need to say, "I won't" to something that is holding you back today?

Where Are You Going?

An army chaplain tells of the time he was asked to preach at a church some 20 miles from the base. He took his family along, but had neglected to tell his six-year-old daughter where they were going. After a few miles on the road, she asked, "Dad, when we get to where we're going, where will we be?" A good question! And one all of us should try to answer for ourselves.

Think of your life's journey. When you get to where you're going, where will you be? One year, five years, or even 20 years from now, if you keep heading in the same direction you are heading and keep doing what you are doing, what will your life look like? Not only vocationally and financially, but what kind of person will you be? Do you have a pretty clear picture of the way you would like things to turn out, or will you be as surprised when it happens as everybody else?

It has been my experience that most people do not spend much time with these questions. But as Henry David Thoreau once said, "In the long run, we only hit what we aim at."

To live aimlessly is to waste this precious gift of life. But to live with direction is to live fully.

P.S.

Does it all seem confusing at times? Like one wit said, "My life has a superb cast, but I can't figure out the plot."

Through It All!

A student was asked to write an essay about the Quakers. He wrote: "The Quakers are very meek, quiet people who never fight or answer back. I think my father is a Quaker. Not my mother."

Some people, like his mother, may be more verbal during conflict. Others may want to quietly mull the problem over a bit before talking about it. But conflict is a natural and even healthy part of relationships. It is especially important to resolve differences with people we care about and, when conflict is handled correctly, it can actually bring us closer together.

Author and counselor, Charlie Shedd, reports getting this note on the kitchen counter after some unresolved conflict with his wife: "Dear Charlie, I hate you. Love, Martha."

What an interesting note! She told him she was angry, but she told him something else, too. She told him that, in spite of her present feelings, she loved him. Through it all, she was saying, she will always love him.

A basic commitment to love one another is the foundation upon which caring relationships are built. When in conflict with those closest to you, that decision to love – through it all – is vital. No technique, no amount of training, however important, will do more to get you through those tough times.

When The World Says, "No!"

When Henry Ward Beecher was a young boy in school, he learned a lesson in self-confidence, which he never forgot. He was called upon to recite in front of the class. He had hardly begun when the teacher interrupted with an emphatic, "No!" He started over and again the teacher thundered, "No!" Humiliated, Henry sat down.

The next boy rose to recite and had just begun when the teacher shouted, "No!" This student, however, kept on with the recitation until he completed it. As he sat down, the teacher responded, "Very good!"

Henry was irritated. "I recited just as he did," he complained to the teacher.

But the instructor replied, "It is not enough to know your lesson, you must be sure. When you allowed me to stop you, it meant that you were uncertain. If all the world says, 'No!' it is your business to say, 'Yes!' and prove it."

The world says, "No!" in a thousand ways:

"No! You can't do that."

"No! You are wrong."

"No! You are too old."

"No! You are too young."

"No! You are too weak."

"No! It will never work."

"No! You don't have the education."

"No! You don't have the background."

"No! You don't have the money."

"No! It can't be done."

And each "No!" you hear has the potential to erode your confidence bit by bit until you quit altogether. Though the world says, "No!" to you today, will you determine to say, "Yes!" and prove it?

P.S.

It was Benjamin Franklin who first said, "The (United States) Constitution only gives people the right to pursue happiness. You have to catch it yourself."

Take The Plunge

"Watch me dive off the high board, Dad," my ten-year-old son called out. I looked up to the ten-foot-high diving board and waited as he stood at the edge, stooped over, arms extended. He had jumped off the high board many times before, but now his nerve seemed to falter as he contemplated streaking through the air headfirst.

The swimming pool was vacated, so he could take his time. "You can do it, Robby," I encouraged. But he couldn't. Not that evening. For 20 minutes he attempted to muster the courage to make the plunge, and he finally gave up when the pool closed for the night.

"I feel disappointed in myself," Robby said on the way home. "I feel terrible. I know I can do it, though. I *know* I can."

He persuaded me to take him swimming again the next evening. Like the night before, we happened to be the only swimmers. "I'm going to do it this time," he said emphatically. "Watch me!"

He climbed the ladder and walked to the end of the board as I watched. Again I encouraged him. Again he hesitated. As the previous night, his nerve failed. It seemed that he would never conquer his fear and leap.

The lifeguards on duty helped me cheer him on. "You can *do* it, Robby," we all exhorted. "Just do it! Don't think about it. Just do it!"

For 30 minutes we encouraged him. For 30 minutes he started and stopped, he leaned and straightened and fought the fear that held him back.

And then it happened. He extended his arms, bent over the edge and fell headfirst into the water! He emerged to the sounds of laughter and congratulations. He *did* it! He finally *did it!* And before he went home, he did it three more times.

Robby learned something about facing his fear that evening. But he learned something else, too. He learned that some things can't be done with less than full commitment. A chasm cannot be leaped in two small jumps and a dive cannot be made a little at a time. Sometimes you just have to *do it.*

Some things require no less than full commitment. What is requiring your full commitment? Will you take the plunge?

P.S.

Life is tough. It takes up all your time, including weekends, and then you die....

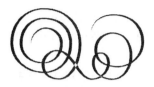

Be Cheerful

A doctor gave a 92-year-old man a physical exam. A few days later he happened to notice the man walking down the street with his arm around a gorgeous young woman and grinning from ear to ear.

The next time he encountered the man, the doctor said, "You are really doing great, aren't you?"

"Just doing what you said, Doc," the man agreed. "You said, 'Get a hot mamma and be cheerful.'"

"I didn't say that," replied the doctor. "I said you got a heart murmur. And be careful."

I wonder if the advice to be cheerful may actually do him more good than to be careful! There is no shortage of self-help books and articles about taking care of yourself physically – from watching your diet to getting proper exercise. In other words, "Be careful!" But just as necessary is learning how to care for your mind and spirit. And cultivating a cheerful attitude can be an important part of the treatment.

Do you tend to focus on what is wrong with your life, or what is right? Are you known as an angry person, or are you known more for being upbeat and positive? Today you can be careful. But will you be cheerful?

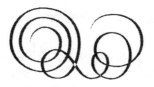

Rise Above

Former U.S. President John F. Kennedy received endless advice and criticism from the media concerning how he should run the country. Much of it he took good-naturedly. In fact, he often used a favorite story in response to the media's comments about how they thought he could do a better job.

He told about a legendary baseball player who always played flawlessly. He consistently hit when at bat and was never thrown out at first. When on base he never failed to score. As a fielder, he never dropped a ball and he threw with unerring accuracy. He ran swiftly and played gracefully.

In fact, he would have been one of the all-time greats except for one thing – no one could ever persuade him to put down his beer and hotdog and come out of the press box to play!

Most of us can empathize, for we all have people in our lives who criticize and second-guess.

They are quick to point out flaws and quicker yet to offer advice.

When it comes to receiving criticism, I believe it helps to remember first that not all criticism is invalid. Wisdom listens for the kernel of truth and saves it for future growth. But when criticism seems unfair, I believe it helps to remember the hawk. When attacked by crows, it does not counterattack. Instead, the hawk soars higher and higher in ever-widening circles until the pests leave it alone.

When there is nothing to learn from criticism, can you rise above it and soar?

P.S.

One unknown sage has said that life is like photography...you use the negative to develop.

Bring Your Umbrella

One summer, a drought threatened the crop in a small town. On a hot and dry Sunday, the village parson told his congregation, "There isn't anything that will save us except to pray for rain. Go home, pray, believe, and come back next Sunday ready to thank God for sending rain."

The people did as they were told and returned to church the following Sunday. But as soon as the parson saw them, he was furious.

"We can't worship today. You do not yet believe," he said.

"But," they protested, "we prayed, and we do believe."

"Believe?" he responded. "Then where are your umbrellas?"

The story applies to all of us. There are those people who leave their umbrellas at home. Throughout their lives, they are merely hoping their wishes and prayers will bear fruit, but they expect little.

Others expect their dreams and desires to come to pass. It is as if they journey through life always prepared for something to happen.

Today, how will you approach that which you are yearning for? Will you expect your prayers and work to bring about hoped-for results? Will you bring your umbrella?

I'll Never Complain Again

Back in the mid-1970s, a man was driving through Arizona and stopped at a gas station in the middle of a torrential downpour. This was in the days of "full-service" gas stations. He sat inside his dry car while a man, who whistled cheerfully while he worked, filled up his tank in that awful rain.

As the customer was leaving, he said apologetically, "I'm sorry to get you out in this weather."

The attendant replied, "It doesn't bother me a bit. When I was fighting in Vietnam I made up my mind in a foxhole one day that if I ever got out of this place alive, I would be so grateful I'd never complain about anything again. And I haven't."

Taking responsibility for our attitudes is part of building a whole and happy life.

P.S.

It was Margaret Lee Runbeck who wisely reminded us that happiness is not a station we arrive at, but a manner of traveling.

Try Something Different

Keep doing the same thing and you will keep getting the same results.

Two men were avid moose hunters. Every year they chartered a plane to take them to the Canadian back country. This year hunting was especially good and in a few days they each bagged a moose. They radioed for their pilot to come pick them up.

When the plane arrived, the pilot took one look at the animals and told the hunters they could not take such a heavy load along.

"But we spent all week hunting for these moose," they protested. "And besides, the pilot we hired last year wasn't worried about the moose's weight."

After much argument, the pilot finally relented and allowed them to load the moose. The heavy plane was only airborne for a few minutes when it lost altitude and crashed into the side of a mountain.

As the men struggled out of the wreckage, one hunter asked, "Where are we?"

His friend answered, "About a mile farther than we got last year."

Keep doing the same thing and you will keep getting the same results. It is true of flying and it is true of living.

What is not working well for you? A habit you are trying to break? A relationship with a parent or spouse or child or friend? What is a source of on-going frustration? Getting around to that project you keep promising to complete? Never having enough money to pay the bills? Running up against the same old walls at work?

The truth is, if you keep doing the same things you will keep getting the same results. So, if you don't like the way things are turning out, something must change. Are you ready to try something different?

A Matter Of Character

In his autobiography *Days of Grace* (Random House Audio, 1993), tennis great Arthur Ashe relates a defining incident that occurred when he was 17 years old. He was playing in a tournament in West Virginia. As was often the case, he was the only contestant of color in the tournament.

One night, some of the kids trashed a cabin. They absolutely destroyed it and then decided to say that Arthur was responsible. The incident was reported in the newspapers; Arthur denied his involvement, but the boys would not change their story. The worst part for Arthur was worrying about what his father would say and do. He eventually made the dreaded phone call.

As he surmised, his father had already learned of the vandalism. His father's tone was grim. He asked Arthur only one question. "Arthur Junior," he asked, "all I want to know is...were you mixed up in that mess?"

Arthur answered, "No, Daddy, I wasn't." His father never asked about it again. Arthur learned that day why he had always been encouraged to tell the truth. There would come a time when he *must* be believed, and this was such a time. Because he had already earned his trust and respect, he knew his father believed him. From that day on he was determined, above all else, to live a life of integrity.

Unfortunately, we find notable examples of modern leaders in every field who give low priority to personal integrity. But we do not need saints – we need people like you. People who will be known for their integrity. People who will determine to be their best selves. People who daily earn the trust and respect of others, regardless of their age or station in life. People who insist on the importance of character.

Our world does not need another saint. But it needs you.

Act On It

A little bear cub was confused about how to walk. "What do I do first?" he asked his mother. "Do I start with my right foot or my left? Or both front feet and then my back feet? Or do I move both feet on one side and then both feet on the other?"

His mother answered, "Just quit thinking and start walking."

She was wise, for things will happen only after we put aside thinking and talking and start doing.

Nolan Bushnell, the founder of Atari, said that everyone who has ever taken a shower has an idea. It's the person who gets out of the shower, dries off and does something about it who makes a difference. Or, as columnist Sydney Harris puts it, "Regret for the things we did can be tempered by time; it is regret for the things we did not do that is inconsolable." One of the most important lessons we can learn is to act on a good idea.

P.S.

It has been accurately pointed out that each one of us is given three jobs when we are born:
1. To live well and fully.
2. To die well and fully.
3. In between, to fix what's broken.

Practice, Practice, Practice

Someone noted that their life and their bank both have something in common – they get out of them about as much as they put in. Which, as far as my bank is concerned, isn't much! But it means I can get a great deal of joy and satisfaction out of life if I am careful about what I put into living.

Gary Player for years was a great competitor in national and international golf tournaments. People constantly said to him, "I'd give anything if I could hit a golf ball like you."

Upon hearing that comment one day, Player responded impatiently: "No, you wouldn't. You'd do anything to hit a golf ball like me, if it were easy! Do your know what you have to do to hit a golf ball like me? You've got to get up at 5:00 every morning, go out to the golf course, and hit a thousand golf balls! Your hands start bleeding, and you walk to the clubhouse and wash the blood off your hands, slap a bandage on it, and go out and hit another thousand golf balls! That is what it takes to hit a golf ball like me!"

His goal was to be at the top of his sport. That lofty dream requires practice, practice and more practice. If your desire, on the other hand, is to excel at living – to give and receive love, to experience joy and to develop fulfilling relationships – then how much of *you* will you put into your dream? These things, too, are possible with practice.

Do you actually practice love, even when you don't feel like it? Do you practice finding joy even when you're unhappy? Do you work at difficult relationships? It is not always easy, but the payoff is worth it!

When Are You Too Old?

When asked how it was that she has lived so long, one 91-year-old woman replied, "I think God is testing the patience of my relatives."

When is "too old"? At what age do we give up? At 100, Grandma Moses was still painting, and Titian painted "Battle of Lepants" when he was 98.

At 93, George Bernard Shaw wrote *Far-fetched Fables*.

At 91, Eamon de Valera served as president of Ireland.

At 90, Pablo Picasso still drew and engraved.

At 89, Arthur Rubinstein gave one of his greatest recitals in New York's Carnegie Hall, and Pablo Casals, at 88, still performed cello concerts.

At 82, Winston Churchill wrote the four-volume work, *A History of the English-Speaking Peoples*, Leo Tolstoy completed *I Cannot Be Silent*, and Goethe, at the same age, finished *Faust*.

At 81, Benjamin Franklin engineered the diplomacy, which led to the adoption of the U.S. Constitution.

When are you "too old"? Only on the day when you truly have nothing left to give. And the good news is this: that day never has to arrive!

P.S.

Senility Prayer

*God, grant me the senility to forget the
people I never liked anyway,
the good fortune to run into the ones I do,
and the eyesight to tell the difference.*

Withstanding Life's Blows

The story isn't true, but it makes a good point. A woman's pet canary sang beautifully and filled her with delight. Until the day she vacuumed the cage.

To her dismay, Pretty Pete was sucked right up into the vacuum cleaner! She opened the bag and dug her hand through dust and dirt until she found the stunned bird, buried alive in a month's worth of filth. To make matters worse, she rushed over to the sink and held him by his little legs under the faucet until he became yellow again!

A few days later a friend asked how Pretty Pete was getting along.

"Oh, I suppose he's doing all right," she said, "except he doesn't sing anymore. He just sits there and stares off into space with a sort of glassy-eyed look on his face."

I have seen that look! And more than once we may have seen it in the mirror. Especially after experiencing a severe blow of some kind.

An old Russian proverb says: "The hammer shatters glass, but forges steel." That is to say, when the hammer of harsh circumstances comes down on you, if you're fragile, you may shatter. But if you have sufficient power and faith, the hammer will forge you into steel.

We are all meant to be steel! Daily, life's blows can actually help us to become more like steel than glass.

Hang On To Each Other

Too often we feel alone. But there is always someone ready to take our hand. There is a beautiful story of an overworked nurse who escorted a tired, young man to her patient's bedside. Leaning over and speaking loudly to the elderly patient, she said, "Your son is here."

With great effort, his unfocussed eyes opened, then flickered shut again. The young man squeezed the aged hand in his and sat beside the bed. Throughout the night he sat there, holding the old man's hand and whispering words of comfort.

By morning's light, the patient had died. In moments, hospital staff swarmed into the room to turn off machines and remove needles. The nurse stepped over to the young man's side and began to offer sympathy, but he interrupted her. "Who was that man?" he asked.

The startled nurse replied, "I thought he was your father!"

41

"No, he was not my father," he answered. "I never saw him before in my life."

"Then why didn't you say something when I took you to him?"

"I realized he needed his son and his son wasn't here," the man explained. "And since he was too sick to recognize that I was not his son, I knew he needed me."

Mother Teresa used to remind us that nobody should have to die alone. Likewise, nobody should have to grieve alone or cry alone either. Or laugh alone or celebrate alone.

We are made to travel life's journey hand in hand. There is someone ready to grasp your hand today. And someone hoping you will take theirs.

P.S.

Rainbows are just to look at, not to really understand. ~ A small child

Courage Of Conviction

Rollo May so accurately asserts that the opposite of courage in our society is not cowardice, but conformity. It takes guts to break from the herd.

Sen. John Tyler was a man who built his life around the courage of his convictions. Consequently, people trusted him enough to elect him President of the United States.

An example of his ability to do what he believed was right, in spite of its unpopularity, occurred once when he was caught up in a critical Senate vote. His vote was the deciding vote and the pressure from his colleagues was tremendous. His name was called and Tyler voted his conscience. He voted against the pressure. Feeling the weight of his vote, he visibly slumped in his seat.

At that moment there was only shocked and unbelieving silence in the great hall. Tyler then arose and walked out, as one writer puts it, "in the proud company of his own self-respect."

He knew that exercising the courage to make those difficult decisions is part of building a life that matters.

The Power Of Laughter

Did you follow the 1987 football season when the Denver Broncos played the Cleveland Browns for the AFC title?

Less than two minutes remained in the game and Cleveland was ahead by a touchdown. The Broncos had just fumbled the ball out of bounds on their own 1/2-yard line. Hostile Cleveland fans were already throwing dog biscuits onto the field and celebrating a sure Cleveland win.

While the announcer was discussing who Cleveland would play in the Super Bowl and Denver fans were nursing bruised egos, the Broncos huddled in their own end zone. Quarterback, John Elway, was known for miraculous wins, but this situation was almost impossible.

All-pro left tackle, Keith Bishop, looked around the huddle at his teammates, took a deep breath and said, "Hey, now we got them right where we want them!" Tense silence was broken by laughter. One player laughed so hard he fell down! Somehow the joke lent perspective to an absurd situation and a sense of calm confidence replaced anxiety.

What followed has been dubbed in the annals of football lore as *The Drive*. In less than two minutes, John Elway and the Broncos drove the length of the field and tied the game with just seconds left. They won in overtime and went on to the 1988 Super Bowl (which, judged by the Broncos' poor showing, was itself a kind of joke...).

An amazing shift occurred in the huddle that day. Laughter prepared them to bring their best to a demanding situation as nervous, negative energy was swept away in the absurdity of the moment.

Laughter has a way of creating positive change in any tense and stressful circumstance. But, as Mark Twain said, laughter is the greatest weapon that we humans possess and it's the one we use the least. Daily, we have countless opportunities to use the power of laughter to make a positive difference.

P.S.

Wasn't it also Mark Twain who said that human beings are the only creatures who can blush – or need to?

Hugging

These words from an unknown author remind us of the importance of physical contact to a relationship.

Hugging is healthy: it helps the body's immune system; it wards off depression; it reduces stress; it induces sleep; it invigorates; it rejuvenates; and it has no unpleasant side effects. Hugging is all natural: it is organic; it is naturally sweet; it contains no pesticides, no preservatives and no artificial ingredients; and it is 100% wholesome. Hugging is practically perfect: there are no movable parts, no batteries to wear out, no periodic checkups; it has low energy consumption and high energy yield; it is inflation-proof; it is non-fattening; it requires no monthly payments and no insurance; it is theft-proof, non-taxable, non-polluting and, of course, fully returnable.

Now, let's go practice!

Friendship

A man complained of loneliness. He was advised to "make three new friends and see what happens."

He later said, "I made three new friends and nothing happened. Now I'm stuck with three new friends!"

Knowing how to *make* friends is helpful. But so is knowing how to *be* a friend. Someone put it well:

Don't walk in front of me – I may not follow.
Don't walk behind me – I may not lead.
Walk beside me – and just be my friend.

Knowing how to be a friend is a vital part of building a whole and happy life.

P.S.

Speaking of friendship, someone observed that the older you get, the tougher it is to lose weight, because by then your body and your fat are really good friends.

Where Change Begins

An old mystic said this about himself: "I was a revolutionary when I was young, and my prayer to God was, 'Lord, give me the strength to change the world.' As I approached middle age and realized that my life was halfway gone without changing a single soul, I changed my prayer to, 'Lord, give me the grace to change all those who come into contact with me, especially my family and friends, and I shall be satisfied.' Now that I am an old man, and my days are numbered, I have begun to see how foolish I have been. Now my one prayer is this, 'Lord, give me the grace to change myself.' If I had prayed that right from the start, I would not have wasted my life."

We can waste years trying to change other people. But we can only really change one person – ourselves. In the end, that is probably enough.

Find The Best

A funny story, which seems to have stood the test of time is about two Catholics, Mike and Pat, who are drinking in a bar across the street from a house of prostitution. They are watching the customers come and go and notice that the minister of the local Methodist church rings the doorbell.

"Wouldn't you know it," says Pat, "those Methodists are all alike."

Then they spot the pastor of the Lutheran church sneaking into the bordello.

"Can you believe those Lutherans?" Mike says. "They must be sex maniacs!"

The rabbi from the town's synagogue is next to knock on the door and Pat comments, "Even the Jews are tempted by the flesh."

Finally Father Riley, their parish priest, rings the doorbell. They watch in amazed silence.

Then Mike turns to Pat and says, "How sad. One of the girls must be sick."

Though we laugh at Pat and Mike, don't we too often judge some people by a harsher set of standards than others? We may sometimes look for and expect the worst from those of a different religion, a different political party, a different race or a different background. Perhaps without our even being aware, they are judged more severely than folks more like "us."

Then on the other hand, we may look for and expect the best from "our own." A good solution is to be so busy finding the best in everybody that we have neither the time nor the heart to judge.

P.S.

There's something to be said for patience. After all, the early bird may get the worm, but it's the second mouse who gets the cheese.

Making Choices

Joseph Henry used to tell a rather strange story about his childhood. His grandmother paid a cobbler to make him a pair of shoes.

The man measured his feet and told Joseph that he could choose between two styles: a rounded toe or a square toe. Little Joseph couldn't decide. It seemed to be such a huge decision; after all, they would become his only pair of shoes for a long time.

The cobbler allowed him to take a couple of days to make up his mind. Day after day, Joseph went into the shop, sometimes three or four times a day! Each time he looked over the cobbler's shoes and tried to decide. The round-toed shoes were more practical, but the square toes looked more fashionable. He continued to procrastinate. He wanted to make up his mind, but he just couldn't decide!

Finally, one day he went into the shop and the cobbler handed him a parcel wrapped in brown paper. His new shoes! He raced home. He tore off the wrapping and found a beautiful pair of leather shoes – one with a rounded toe and the other with a square toe!

Joseph learned a difficult lesson about decisions: if we don't make them ourselves, others will make them for us. And wholeness in life can only come about when we take full responsibility for the choices we make.

Dream Something Beautiful

A mother of a vivacious five-year-old just returned from a meeting of the National Organization for Women. Stirred by exciting dreams for the possibilities of womanhood, she asked her daughter what she wanted to be when she grew up. Little Lisa quickly answered, "A nurse."

There was a time when nursing was thought of as a woman's profession and the answer somehow seemed not to satisfy. She had, after all, just returned from a NOW conference.

"You can be *anything* you want to be," she reminded her daughter. "You can be a lawyer, a surgeon, a banker, president of the country – you can be anything."

"Anything?" Lisa asked.

"Anything!" her mother smiled.

"I know," Lisa said. "I want to be a *horse!*"

Lisa's dream may need some refinement, but there is plenty of time for that. When do we quit dreaming about the future? When do we resign ourselves to simply replaying dreams from the past?

Maybe her dream needs to mature a bit, but would you rather have the optimism of a five-year-old girl who wants to be a horse, or the pessimism of an adult who says in despair, "I can't be anything at all"?

Teddy Roosevelt said, "Keep your eyes on the stars and your feet on the ground." That's the way to make those dreams come true. It begins with looking up and dreaming something beautiful.

P.S.

If you encounter resistance as you pursue your dreams, remember that for every action there is an equal and opposite criticism.

What Do You Pray For?

I often remember something Mahatma Gandhi said about courage. He was a leader in India's struggle for independence, a man who is remembered for bringing the British Empire to its knees without firing a shot.

Speaking about the source of his courage, he once related a story about an incident, which occurred in South Africa. There was a law directed expressly against Indians in South Africa that he had gone there to oppose. His ship was met by a hostile mob that had come with the announced intention of lynching him. Gandhi was advised to stay on board for his own physical safety. But he went ashore nevertheless.

When later asked why he made such a dangerous decision, he explained, "I was stoned and kicked and beaten a good deal; but I had not prayed for safety, but for the courage to face the mob, and that courage came and did not fail me."

Do you pray only for safety and health and protection? Or also for the courage to face whatever may come? In the end, your health will finally flee, and hope for deliverance from harm, disease and even death will disappoint. But when you seek power to face whatever life brings, that courage will come and not fail you.

Unstoppable

When a group of two hundred executives were asked what makes a person successful, eighty percent listed enthusiasm as the most important quality. More important than skill. More important than training. Even more important than experience.

Before water will produce enough steam to power an engine, it must boil. The steam engine won't move a train an inch until the steam gauge registers 212 degrees. Likewise, the person without enthusiasm is trying to move the machinery of life with lukewarm water. Only one thing will happen: that person will stall.

A. B. Zu Tavern asserts that enthusiasm is electricity in the battery. It's the vigor in the air. It's the warmth in the fire. It's the breath in all things alive. Successful people are enthusiastic about what they do. "Good work is never done in cold blood," he says. "Heat is needed to forge anything. Every great achievement is the story of a flaming heart."

You may have sufficient skill, training and experience. Add enthusiasm to those assets and you will be truly unstoppable!

P.S.

*Sign on boss's wall: All workers will be fired with enthusiasm, or else they will be fired – **with enthusiasm!***

Copy This!

A true story points to a universal truth about human beings: we learn best by imitation. President Calvin Coolidge once invited friends from his hometown to dine with him at the White House. Unsure of their table manners, the guests decided to imitate the president. They watched closely to see which utensils he used, what foods he ate and when.

Their strategy seemed to succeed until coffee was served. Coolidge poured some coffee into his saucer. They did the same. He added sugar and cream. His guests did, too. Then the president bent over and put his saucer on the floor for the cat!

Like Coolidge's hometown guests, we, too, seem to learn best by imitation. Kids learn by observing parents when they are young, and by copying their peers, as they grow older. They learn by observing television and movie characters as readily as the lives of actual people. Adults learn best by modeling a personality trait or skill in another, which they want to adopt.

Perhaps you want to develop better social skills. Or maybe you want to learn how to organize, how to sell a product or relate to a child. Just about *any* trait or skill can be learned: find it in someone and copy it. And the best part is – you can do it today.

Attitude Determines Altitude

Unlike some things in life, we can choose our outlook. Sometimes we just need a reminder that happiness can often simply be a result of choosing attitudes:

I woke up early today, excited over all I get to do before the clock strikes midnight. I have responsibilities to fulfill today. My job is to choose what kind of day I am going to have.

Today I can complain because the weather is rainy or I can be thankful that the grass is getting watered for free.

Today I can feel sad that I don't have more money or I can be glad that my finances encourage me to plan my purchases wisely and guide me away from waste.

Today I can grumble about my health or I can rejoice that I am alive.

Today I can lament over all that my parents didn't give me when I was growing up or I can feel grateful that they allowed me to be born.

Today I can cry because roses have thorns or I can celebrate that thorns have roses.

Today I can mourn my lack of friends or I can excitedly embark upon a quest to discover new relationships.

Today I can whine because I have to go to work or I can shout for joy because I have a job to do.

Today I can complain because I have to go to school or eagerly open my mind and fill it with rich new tidbits of knowledge.

Today I can murmur dejectedly because I have to do housework or I can feel honored because God has provided shelter for my mind, body, and soul.

Today stretches ahead of me, waiting to be shaped. And here I am, the sculptor who gets to do the shaping. What today will be like is up to me.

I get to choose what kind of day I will have!
(Author unknown)

P.S.

Good attitudes are especially hard to find around tax time. One tax auditor says, "The trick is to stop thinking of it as 'your' money."

I Always Wanted To!

An old prospector wandered into a small town where he was accosted by a loud, obnoxious and quite drunken cowboy. The cowboy pointed his six-shooters in the old miner's direction and asked, "Old man, do you know how to dance?"

"Nope," the prospector replied.

"Maybe you'd better learn," said the cowpuncher. Hot lead kicked up dust around the old man's feet and he began to dance.

Soon, however, the guns were empty. The old prospector reached into his saddlebag and pulled out a sawed-off shotgun.

"Son," he said, "you ever kissed a mule?" Looking first at the shotgun, then at the spot where the mule's tail is attached to its body, the young cowboy got the message.

"Nope," he answered, "I never kissed a mule. But I always *wanted* to!"

In real life, desire is not something that can be given by anyone else! It comes from the inside. Nobody can make us *want* anything important. If we decide we want to improve, if we want meaningful relationships or more fulfilling work, if we want rich spiritual lives or healthier bodies, then the desire must come from our own hearts. Nobody can make us *want* those things. And, at the same time, nothing important will ever happen without sufficient desire.

It's said that "want power makes will power." If you want it badly enough, you will find a way to make it happen. But look within for "want power." Because that is where it is to be found. And sufficient desire is the necessary first step to accomplishing anything worthwhile.

A Climate Of Forgiveness

In his tape *Living Faith* (Random House Audio Books, 1996), President Jimmy Carter shares that forgiveness is fundamental to his life. He says that without the knowledge that he can be forgiven, it would be impossible for him to face his own shortcomings. This even includes forgiveness of himself.

He relates that both he and his wife, Rosalynn, are "strong-willed" persons who find it difficult to admit being at fault.

One day, after a particularly disturbing argument, Carter decided that he would never let another day end with each of them angry with the other. So he went out to his wood shop and cut a thin piece of walnut, a little smaller than a bank check. On it, he carved the words, "Each evening forever this is good for an apology or forgiveness, as you desire." That evening, he gave the plaque to Rosalynn. He reports that, so far, he has been able to honor it each time Rosalyn has presented it to him.

With his plaque, Carter created a climate of forgiveness between the two of them. Without the knowledge that we will be forgiven, how quickly will we admit our own faults? And how can our closest relationships be healthy if we are each afraid to apologize or unwilling to accept an apology? A climate of forgiveness is a necessary part of happiness.

P.S.

Speaking of forgiveness, someone accurately pointed out that a friend is one who, when we make a complete fool of ourselves, doesn't believe it's a permanent job!

The Next Step

Weary of constantly picking clothes up from the floor of her son's room, a mother finally laid down the law: each item of clothing she had to pick up would cost her son 25 cents. By the end of the week, he owed her $1.50. She received the money promptly, along with a 50-cent tip and a note that read, "Thanks, Mom; keep up the good work!"

I suppose he found a painless way around the problem! He also found a way around disciplining himself. Of course, picking up his room was probably her goal, not his, but, like all responsible parents, she was trying to teach him the value of self-discipline.

Although most people do have goals, few of them have actually made realistic plans to reach their goals. And only two or three percent will have the self-discipline to implement their plans.

What are you trying to accomplish? Will you take the next step today?

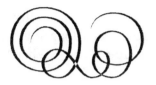

True Love

How easy it is to confuse love with passion! One father said of his teenaged son, "I don't know if he's in love or in heat!" Feelings of attraction can change more quickly than the seasons, but love, in its truest form, is greater than feelings.

Love is what Mr. and Mrs. Strauss shared. Mrs. Isadore Strauss was one of the few first class women passengers to go down with the *Titanic* in 1912, and she drowned because she could not bear to leave her husband.

They remained calm throughout the excitement of the sinking vessel. They both aided frightened women and children to find places aboard lifeboats. Finally, Mr. Strauss, who had repeatedly urged his wife to claim a spot safely aboard a lifeboat, forced her to enter one.

She was seated but a moment, however, when she sprang up and climbed back on deck before he could stop her. There, she caught his arm, snuggling it familiarly against her side, and exclaimed, "We have been long together for a great many years. We are old now. Where you go, I will go."

For them, true love was about commitment. And it was about faithfulness. And sacrifice. Not everyone finds such love in another person – though it is a beautiful thing when it occurs. But a committed and faithful love can always be found in another realm. It exists at the very core of authentic spirituality. This is a fact that whole and happy people build their lives around.

P.S.

Regina (age 10) says, "I'm not rushing into being in love. I'm finding the fourth grade hard enough."

Eight Gifts That Don't Cost A Cent

This simple checklist can help measure how you are nurturing your relationships.

The Gift of Listening
But you must *really* listen. Don't interrupt, don't daydream, don't plan your response. Just listen.

The Gift of Affection
Be generous with appropriate hugs, kisses, pats on the back and handholds. Let these small actions demonstrate the love you have for family and friends.

The Gift of Laughter
Clip cartoons. Share articles and funny stories. Your gift will say, "I love to laugh with you."

The Gift of Solitude

There are times when we want nothing better than to be left alone. Be sensitive to those times and give the gift of solitude to others.

The Gift of a Favor
Every day, go out of your way to do something kind.

The Gift of a Written Note
It can be a simple "Thanks for the help" note or a full sonnet. A brief, handwritten note may be remembered for a lifetime.

The Gift of a Compliment
A simple and sincere, "You look great in red," "You did a super job," or "That was a wonderful meal" can make someone's day.

The Gift of a Cheerful Disposition
The easiest way to feel good is to extend a kind word to someone. *(Author unknown)*

Those who take care of their relationships build whole and happy lives.

Do It Today

A true story is told of a woman from Switzerland who was served dinner on a domestic American flight. She immediately opened up her dessert – a delicious looking piece of chocolate cake – and heavily salted and peppered it. The flight attendant was shocked and said to the passenger, "Oh! It's not necessary to do that!"

"But it *is*," the woman replied, smiling. "It keeps me from eating it!"

She found a way to remove temptation! In other areas of life, however, temptation is not so easily removed. We may be tempted to forgo some much-needed exercise because we "just don't feel like it" today. Or we may allow a persistent habit or addiction to take over, even though we have been "wanting to quit." Or we may never get around to that reading program we have meant to start, or to signing up for that class or those music lessons. We may *want* to do these things; it's just that we give in to the temptation to put it off!

Is there a better day than today to do that thing you *really* want to do?

P.S.

Speaking of temptation, someone pointed out that opportunity knocks only once, but temptation bangs on our door for years!

Time Well-Spent

Charles Francis Adams was the United States ambassador to Great Britain during the Lincoln administration. He had the habit of keeping a daily diary. He also taught his son, Brooks, the value of journaling his activities in a diary.

One memorable day, eight-year-old Brooks recorded, "Went fishing with my father, the most glorious day of my life." It must have been, for the next forty years Brooks repeatedly mentioned it in his diary.

His father also wrote about the fishing trip. His own diary on that pivotal day for his son reads, "Went fishing with my son; a day wasted."

Did he ever know that a single day spent with Brooks may have been the most well spent day of his life? He may have felt that, as a United States ambassador, his time was extremely valuable. But history seems to show that some individual time spent with his son may have turned out to be one of his most valuable investments. Which raises the question...is there an important way you can spend some time today?

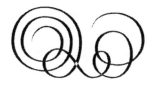

Embrace Change

We live in an age when it seems that almost *anything* is possible! Imagine receiving an e-mail halfway around the globe that was written only minutes before!

A clerk at a Philadelphia airline counter picked up the telephone and heard the caller ask, "How long does it take to go from Philadelphia to Phoenix?"

She was busy with another customer just then and intended to put the caller on hold.

"Just a minute," she replied.

As she was about the press the "Hold" button, the clerk heard the caller say, "Thank you," and hang up!

Our world changes so quickly we may think that most anything is possible. I heard someone mention that he believes that most of the changes that will ever take place already have occurred. I don't think so. Our new reality is one of constant change.

Some changes can be very good, such as medical advances and technological breakthroughs. But most change is uncomfortable at first.

Do you resist our quickly changing world, longing for the past? Or do you embrace change and adapt with it? With all of its changes, the world can still be a wonderful and exciting place to live. Your attitude toward change is an important part of determining whether you can be happy.

P.S.

Douglas Adams helps us to keep everything in perspective. He says, "There is a theory which states that if ever anyone discovers exactly what the universe is for and why it is here, it will instantly be replaced by something even more bizarre and inexplicable. There is another theory which states that has already happened."

Thankfulness

I understand that the late Dr. Fulton Oursler used to tell of an old woman who took care of him when he was a child. Anna was a former slave who, after emancipation, was hired by the family for many years.

He remembered her sitting at the kitchen table, her hands folded and her eyes gazing upward as she prayed, "Much obliged, Lord, for my vittles." He asked her what vittles were and she replied that they were food and drink. He told her that she would get food and drink whether or not she gave thanks, and Anna said, "Yes, we'll get our vittles, but it makes 'em taste better when we're thankful."

She told him that an old preacher taught her, as a little girl, to always look for things to be grateful for. So, as soon as she awoke each morning, she asked herself, "What is the first thing I can be grateful for today?" Sometimes the smell of early-morning coffee perking in the kitchen found its way to her room. On those mornings, the aroma prompted her to say, "Much obliged, Lord, for the coffee. And much obliged, too, for the smell of it!"

Young Fulton grew up and left home. One day he received a message that Anna was dying. He returned home and found her in bed with her hands folded over her white sheets, just as he had seen them folded in prayer over her white apron at the kitchen table so many times before.

He wondered what she could give thanks for at a time like this. As if reading his mind, she opened her eyes and gazed at the loving faces around her bed. Then, shutting her eyes again, she said quietly, "Much obliged, Lord, for such fine friends."

Oursler was deeply influenced by Anna's uncanny ability to always find something to be thankful for. This wise woman taught him a vital secret that many people have never learned: she taught him how to be happy.

Who Packs Your Parachute?

Who packs your parachute? Charles Plumb was a U.S. Naval Academy graduate who flew jets in Vietnam. After 75 combat missions, he was shot down by a surface-to-air missile. He ejected and parachuted into the jungle. The Vietcong captured him and held him prisoner for six years in North Vietnam. Today, Charles Plumb lectures on lessons learned from that experience.

One day, when he and his wife were sitting in a restaurant, a man at another table came over and said, "You're Plumb! You flew jet fighters in Vietnam from the aircraft carrier Kitty Hawk. You were shot down!"

"How in the world did you know that?" asked the former pilot.

"I packed your parachute!" he said. Plumb gasped in surprise. The man pumped his hand and said, "I guess it worked!"

Plumb assured him it did. "If your chute hadn't worked, I wouldn't be here today."

The pilot couldn't sleep that night, thinking about the stranger. He wondered how many times he might have seen him and not spoken because he was a fighter pilot and the man who packed his chute was "just a sailor." Plumb thought of the many hours the sailor had spent on a long wooden table in the bowels of the ship, carefully weaving the shrouds and folding the silks of each chute, holding in his hands each time the fate of someone he didn't know.

When Plumb lectures, he asks his audience, "Who's packing your parachute?" A good question, for we all have someone who provides, and has provided, what we need to get through our lives. We need physical parachutes, mental parachutes, emotional parachutes, and spiritual parachutes.

Who has taught you that much-valued skill, or broadened your mind, or helped you find emotional healing, or put you in touch with spiritual values? Throughout your life, who has been packing your parachute? These are the people we owe our lives to. And whose parachutes are you packing? For that is the legacy you will leave behind.

P.S.

Children were asked, "How can a stranger tell if two people are married?" Eddie, age six, said, "Married people usually look happy to talk to other people." Eight-year-old Derrick said, "You might have to guess based on whether they seem to be yelling at the same kids."

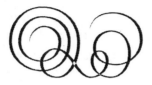

Dare To Trust

You may remember the old story of two men who ordered beers in a bar. One of them threw down some bottle caps in payment.

"What's this?" asked the bartender.

The other man motioned him aside and said in hushed tones, "That's my uncle. He's a little confused. Just humor him, okay? Then I'll settle up with you later."

The server agreed and the men continued drinking beer until the bartender finally came over and said to the second man, "It's closing time. How about settling up with me now."

"How many bottle caps do you have?" the guy asked.

"Twenty-four."

"Fair enough," he replied. "Do you have change for a manhole cover?"

Though the story is silly, it raises the question of whom we can trust. In business, we may get "stiffed." In love, we may get "burned." Even good friends may let you down; lovers may betray; strangers may disappoint. So do we simply decide never to trust? Or is never trusting a no-fail recipe for misery?

The truth is, a healthy and happy life can *only* thrive in an atmosphere of trust. Truly happy people know that trust is as essential as the air they breathe. They believe that friends *can* also be counted on, lovers *do* show faith, and strangers *will* often come through.

And the truth is, they are usually right!

Great Teachers

Computers and technology made Ross Perot a wealthy man. But his greatest teacher was not a university professor or a computer expert. It was his mother – who raised him before the phrase "computer age" was ever coined.

He remembers the little things she did which taught him to be the kind of man he eventually became. Like showing generosity and compassion.

During the Great Depression, "hoboes" regularly knocked on their door asking for a little food. One day one of these visitors told his mother why. Out on the curb in front of their house an earlier hobo had placed a white mark, indicating to later travelers that their house was an "easy mark." Young Ross asked his mother if she wanted him to erase the white mark. She told him to leave it there. He never forgot that tiny act of compassion.

Ross Perot believed he received his greatest learnings from his mother. Her lessons were the kind he could never pick up in a school. Her influence in shaping his life was beyond measure.

You, too, are teaching powerful lessons simply by the way you live.

P.S.

Is your life more like an exclamation, or an explanation?

One Of The Ten!

On her 50th wedding anniversary, a woman revealed the secret of her long and happy marriage. She said, "On my wedding day, I decided to make a list of ten of my husband's faults which, for the sake of the marriage, I would overlook."

One of her guests asked her what some of the faults she chose to overlook were. "To tell you the truth," she replied, "I never did get around to making that list. But whenever my husband did something that made me hopping mad, I would say to myself, 'Lucky for him that's one of the ten!'"

She never created the list, but she created something else over the years – an attitude of understanding. And that goes a long way in building a whole and happy life.

A Second Chance

Mayor Anthony Williams of Washington D.C. has a remarkable story. Williams was born to an unwed teen who gave him up. He was known as a "problem child" in foster care. By age three, Anthony had still never spoken a word. It seemed that a pattern for his life was set, that is, until two warm and caring people took a chance on him.

Anthony was taken in by an opera-singing postal clerk and her equally generous-hearted husband. He soon began to speak and eventually thrived in their home. He excelled academically and later attended both Harvard and Yale Universities.

In 1998, he came from obscurity to win 66% of the vote to become mayor in one of the world's major cities. In his inaugural address, Williams said: "Forty-four years ago, my parents adopted me and gave me a second chance. I feel this city has now adopted me and I will give to it everything my

parents taught me about love, service, commitment."

He was saved by a second chance. And in
smaller, yet significant ways, we, too, have been
given second chances.

Likewise, we, too, have abundant opportunities to give them. Today may be the day to take
that chance – and give a second chance.

P.S.

It has been beautifully said that God won't always remove the darkness, but will accompany us through it.

Unconditional Love

An unknown author beautifully portrays the possibilities of unconditional love in this heartfelt gesture.

The Rock

As she grew older her teenage daughter became increasingly rebellious. It culminated late one night when the police arrested her daughter for drunk driving. Mom had to go to the police station to pick her up.

They didn't speak until the next afternoon. Mom broke the tension by giving her a small gift-wrapped box. Her daughter nonchalantly opened it and found a little rock inside.

She rolled her eyes and said, "Cute, Mom, what's this for?"

"Read the card," Mom instructed.

Her daughter took the card out of the envelope and read it. Tears started to trickle down her cheeks. She got up and lovingly hugged her mom as the card fell to the floor.

On the card were these words: "This rock is more than 200,000,000 years old. That is how long it will take before I give up on you."

Anything less than 200,000,000 years is simply giving up too quickly!

Learn How To Stoop

Is it possible to be both humble and emotionally healthy?

One young man acquired a job in a grocery store. On the first day of work, the manager handed him a broom and said, "I want you to sweep the floor."

Stunned, the new employee said, "But I'm a college graduate!"

"Oh, I'm sorry," replied the boss, "I didn't know. Here then, give me the broom and I'll show you how."

He wouldn't stoop that low! He had risen above sweeping. But one of life's peculiar lessons is that in occasionally *lowering* ourselves we find true contentment. We sometimes believe that if we can only rise to a particular standard of living, or if we can rise above a certain income level, or ascend to a certain educational level that we will be happy. But we are never all that happy until we learn the values of *simplicity* and *service*. It's a matter also of lowering ourselves – learning how to stoop!

It is as if life's gifts are all on shelves, one above the other. But the greatest gifts are on the lowest shelves, one *beneath* the other. So it is by *stooping* lower, always going down, that we get the best gifts!

P.S.

Good judgment comes from experience, and a lot of that comes from bad judgment.

Make A Difference

Do you ever think that one person really doesn't matter? Tabitha Brown proved that one person *does* matter.

It was 1846. She joined one of the wagon trains of adventurers hoping to start a life in America's west.

Grandma Brown, as she was affectionately called, was 62 years old, only five feet tall, and weighed all of 108 pounds when well fed. Because she was partly paralyzed, she leaned on a cane and walked with a limp.

Along the way, she showed great courage and stamina. As she crossed the Great Plains and the Rocky Mountains, she nursed the wagon train's sick, though at one point, she neared starvation herself after the caravan's cattle were rustled off by Rogue River Indians.

Once they arrived in Oregon, she started one of the first schools in that part of the country. It was for all people, both rich and poor. The poor attended free while those who could afford paid a dollar a week for tuition and board.

As long as she was able, she worked to keep the institution alive. She attended to the students. She convinced would-be faculty of the need for teachers at the school. Many days found Grandma Brown hobbling about on her lame leg in the kitchen, kneading and baking the necessary daily bread.

And by the way, *one person can make a difference*. Today, that institution is known as Pacific University.

P.S.

One survivor said, "Insanity is my only means of relaxation."

Meant To Be One

In 1942, the American consul ordered citizens home from the Persian Gulf, for fear they might get caught in the spreading conflict of World War II.

Travel was difficult, and some civilians secured passage on the troop ship *Mauritania*. Passengers included thousands of Allied soldiers, 500 German prisoners of war, and 25 civilian women and children.

The ship traveled slowly and cautiously, constantly in danger from hostile submarines patrolling the ocean depths. It was Christmas Eve and they had traveled for a full two months. They had only made it as far as the coastal waters of New Zealand, and everyone on board was homesick, anxious and frightened.

Someone came up with the idea of asking the captain for permission to sing Christmas carols for the German prisoners, who were surely as homesick and lonely as the passengers. Permission was granted.

A small choral group made its way to the quarters where the unsuspecting prisoners were held. They decided to sing "Silent Night" first, as it was written in Germany by Joseph Mohr and was equally well known by the prisoners.

Within seconds of beginning the carol, a deafening clatter shook the floor. Hundreds of German soldiers sprang up and crowded the tiny windows in order to better see and hear the choristers. Tears streamed unashamedly down their faces. At that moment, everyone on both sides of the wall experienced the universal truth – *that all people everywhere are one.*

Hope and love broke down the barriers between warring nations and, for that moment at least, all were one family. We are meant to be one. And in that knowledge we find true peace.

Un-thanked People

When William Stidger taught at Boston University, he once reflected upon the great number of un-thanked people in his life. Those who had helped nurture him, inspire him or who cared enough about him to leave a lasting impression.

One was a schoolteacher he'd not heard of in many years. But he remembered that she had gone out of her way to put a love of verse in him, and Will had loved poetry all his life. He wrote a letter of thanks to her.

The reply he received, written in the feeble scrawl of the aged, began, "My dear Willie." He was delighted. Now over 50, bald and a professor, he didn't think there was a person left in the world who would call him "Willie." Here is that letter:

My dear Willie,
I cannot tell you how much your note meant to me. I am in my eighties, living alone in a small

room, cooking my own meals, lonely and, like the last leaf of autumn, lingering behind. You will be interested to know that I taught school for 50 years and yours is the first note of appreciation I ever received. It came on a blue-cold morning and it cheered me as nothing has in many years.

Not prone to cry easily, Will wept over that note. She was one of the *great un-thanked people* from Will's past. You know them. We all do. The teacher who made a difference. That coach we'll never forget. The music instructor or Sunday school worker who helped us to believe in ourselves. That scout leader who cared.

We all remember people who shaped our lives in various ways. People whose influence changed us. Will Stidger found a way to show his appreciation – he wrote them letters.

Who are some of the un-thanked people from your past? It may not be too late to say, "Thanks."

P.S.

Whether or not love makes the world go around, it usually makes the ride worth-while.

An Encouraging Word

A young Polish boy wanted to play piano, but his teacher told him that his fingers were too stubby and that he would never play well. The boy was advised to try the cornet, but was later told by an expert musician that he did not have the lip to ever be good.

Then one day he met the great pianist, Anton Rubinstein. The famous musician gave this young boy the first bit of encouragement he ever received. "Young man," Rubinstein said, "you might be able to play the piano. In fact, I think you can...if you will practice seven hours a day."

That was all the encouragement he needed! The great Rubinstein had told him he *could do it!* He would have to dedicate his life to practicing piano, but he *could do it!* He could be *good!* Anton Rubinstein said so!

He *did* practice for many hours a day and his hard work was rewarded; for years later, Jan Pad-

117

erewski became one of the most famous pianists of his time. An encouraging word carried within it the power to ignite a young boy's eager spirit, which burned brightly for decades.

Your encouraging word, given today, may forever change a receptive life!

True Prayer

I asked God to take away my pride. God said, "No. It is not for me to take away, but for you to give it up."

I asked God to make my handicapped child whole. God said, "No. Her spirit is whole, her body is only temporary."

I asked God to grant me patience. God said, "No. Patience is a by-product of tribulations; it isn't granted, it is earned."

I asked God to give me happiness. God said, "No. I give you blessings, happiness is up to you."

I asked God to spare me pain. God said, "No. Suffering draws you apart from worldly cares and brings you closer to me."

I asked God to make my spirit grow. God said, "No. You must grow on your own, but I will prune you to make you fruitful."

I asked for all things that I might enjoy life. God said, "No. I will give you life so that you may enjoy all things."

*I asked God to help me **love** others, as much as God loves me. God said... "Ahhhh, finally you have the idea!" (Author unknown)*

Someone accurately said that maturity in prayer occurs when we are able to move from the plea, "Give me..." to the deeper prayer, "Use me."

P.S.

The optimist believes that we live in the best of all possible worlds. The pessimist is afraid the optimist might be right....

Laugh About It!

I recently read of a motorist who was caught in an automated speed trap. His speed was measured by a radar machine and his car was automatically photographed. In a few days he received a ticket for $40 in the mail along with a picture of his automobile. As payment, he sent the police department a snapshot of $40. Several days later, he received a letter from the police. It contained another picture – of handcuffs!

Humor is an important part of a healthy life. Though often under-used, humor is also an essential problem-solving tool, particularly in conflict. It goes a long way toward building bridges over divisive waters. What might happen if you use humor to get at that aggravating problem you are facing today?

P.S.

You think you've got it bad? According to Merlyn Cundiff, a tourist in Las Vegas didn't have money to gamble, so he watched games and bet mentally. In no time at all, he'd lost his mind.

Leave The Past

Are you ever disturbed by memories? Wouldn't it be nice to simply click the delete key and erase the pain while leaving only happy recollections?

I like the story of the minister who passed along to a beginning pastor a trick he used when he noticed the congregation nodding off.

"I suddenly say to them, 'Last night I held another man's wife in my arms.' And, when everyone sits up shocked, I continue, 'It was my own dear mother.'"

The young preacher liked it and was ready the following Sunday when most of his congregation was drowsing. He said in a loud voice, "You know, last night I held another man's wife in my arms."

Stunned, the congregation sat bolt upright and stared. Unnerved, the young preacher stammered, "Oh dear – I've forgotten who she was."

Have you ever wanted to take back an embarrassing moment, a hasty decision, or a word spoken in the heat of anger? The problem is, some things can't be taken back! Some hurts cannot be undone. And unfortunately, no delete key can correct the past so that memories no longer hurt, frighten or humiliate.

The past is what it is – past. And that, too, is good to remember. It is past. Over. Finished. There is no taking it back, yet no purpose is served in reliving and rehashing old memories. It is gone. Let it be a teacher. Let us learn from its harsh lessons as well as its joys. Then let us leave it where it belongs – in the past.

Today...can you put the past in the past?

Do What You Love

In his book *Asimov Laughs Again* (New York: Harper Collins Publishers, 1993), author Isaac Asimov relates an incident when he was interviewed by television journalist Barbara Walters.

She asked him how many books he had written and then asked, "Don't you ever want to do anything but write?"

He said, "No."

She pressed on. "Don't you want to go hunting? Fishing? Dancing? Hiking?"

This time he answered, "No! No! No! And no!"

She continued, "But what would you do if the doctor gave you only six months to live?"

He said, "Type faster."

Isaac Asimov spent his life doing what he loved. It was comedian George Burns who once said, "I honestly think it is better to be a failure at something you love than to be a success at something you hate."

Easily said, but leaving the safety of what is known and venturing into the unknown can be one of the scariest decisions we can make. And also one of the most fulfilling.

If you no longer find satisfaction in what you do, is it time to leave the familiar behind and follow your heart?

P.S.

Speaking of doing what you hate, one man said, "I've used up all my sick days, so I'm calling in dead."

Move Beyond Failure

It's said, "If at first you don't succeed, give up; failure may be your thing."

I love the humor, but I don't believe the sentiment for a moment! Everyone fails. And sometimes in a big way! But it's also true that courage, persistence, faith, and self-confidence can build a mansion on the rubble left by our greatest failures.

You don't have to follow American football to appreciate that, in 1955, Johnny Unitas failed his first qualifying test to play football with the Pittsburgh Steelers. Once on the team, he fumbled three times during his first regular-season game as quarterback. Each of those fumbles, as well as an interception he threw that game, resulted in a touchdown for the other team. But just fifteen years later, in the 1970 commemoration of the fiftieth anniversary of the National Football League, Johnny Unitas was selected as the greatest quarterback of all time, and the same year the Associated Press named him the outstanding professional football player of the decade.

What happened? He didn't give in to failure. He made a decision to move on after each defeat. After all, every disappointment presents us with two options: to move on or to quit. And how you decide, in the long run, means everything.

Slow Down

An American racing enthusiast entered his horse in Britain's famous Epsom Downs Steeplechase. Just before the race began, he slipped his horse a white pellet. The Duke of Marlboro, who was serving as steward, caught the owner in the act and objected. "I say, old man, really you can't do that sort of thing over here!"

"Just a harmless sugar lump," the American assured him. He gulped one down himself. "Here, try one," he said.

The Duke took a pill, swallowed it, and seemed satisfied. As the jockey mounted, the American whispered in his ear, "Son, keep that horse on the outside and stay out of trouble, because once he starts running, there ain't nothing that can catch him...except me and the Duke of Marlboro!"

Do you ever feel that way – running so fast that nothing can catch you? Our busy and full lives are too often like that; we rush here and hurry there.

We eat fast food. We run our errands. We use e-mail and put off reading our messages until we have the time. We hurry through meals and can only give friends "just a minute." We live fast-paced and anxious lives. Too often, we run so fast we lose our center.

But, in the end, it's not how fast you lived that matters, but how well you lived. Are you taking time to enjoy? Have you left enough time for you? Is there time to listen to a friend or visit a relative in need? Are you leaving time each day to nurture your faith? Do you need to slow down? After all, the only race that matters goes, not to those who run it quickly, but to those who run it well.

P.S.

Ever had trouble knowing where to start? I like what Stephen Bayne said, "I am rather like a mosquito in a nudist camp: I know what I ought to do but don't know where to begin."

Stick Together

An old story is told of two men who went fishing in a small boat. The day was uneventful until one of them hooked a huge fish, which, in the struggle, pulled him overboard! He couldn't swim and began to panic.

"Help!" he yelled. "Save me!"

The friend reached over and grabbed the man by the hair to pull him closer to the boat. But when he tugged, the man's toupee came off and he slipped down under the water again.

He came up shouting, "Hey, help me! I can't swim!"

So the friend reached down again and this time latched onto the struggling man's arm. But when he pulled, the arm came off! It was an artificial limb.

The drowning man continued to kick and thrash around and his friend reached out a third time. This time he grabbed a leg and pulled. You guessed it – he pulled off a wooden leg!

The man continued splashing and sputtering and calling out, "Help me!" and the friend finally called back in disgust, "How can I help you if you won't stick together?"

Similarly, how can people in marriages and families be helped when they won't stick together? How can churches, schools and businesses get anywhere when they won't stick together? And how can a nation function well when it can't stick together?

None of us lives in isolation. This life is a group outing. And some conflict along the way is inevitable. But when we stick together, beautiful things can happen.

If you feel as if things in your life are falling apart, maybe it is because the people in your life are not sticking together!

You're Not Alone

"The commonest and subtlest of all human diseases," a prominent physician said, "is fear." Fear is an incapacitating, paralyzing disease. We all fear at times, but many carry with them unnecessary and destructive fears.

We're afraid of the unknown.

We're afraid of old age; afraid of growing senile and dependent.

We're afraid of change; afraid to plunge into that new relationship, job or way of life.

We're afraid of the future.

We're afraid to risk; afraid to fail or appear as if we failed.

We're afraid to love; afraid to trust.

We're afraid of closeness; afraid we might get hurt.

We're afraid to die. Like Henry Van Dyke said, "Some people are so afraid to die that they never begin to live."

Fear is the most devastating enemy of human personality.

But here's the good news: unnecessary fears can be conquered! Courage to meet fear head-on is actually at our fingertips.

An American slavery abolitionist, Wendell Phillips, made an interesting observation. He noted that it is easy to be brave when all are behind you and agree with you. But the difficulty comes when 99 percent of your friends think you are *wrong*. Then it is the brave soul who stands up – one among 1,000 – remembering that one with God makes a majority!

You see, courage often comes from simply knowing you are not alone.

P.S.

Never be afraid to try something new. Remember, the Ark was built by amateurs; the Titanic was built by professionals.

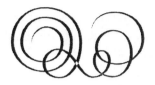

Take Action

One golfer had an absolutely horrible day at the links. His ball lay on an anthill and he swung viciously with a five-iron. Again and again he missed the ball and chopped away at the hill, killing ants and sending sand flying through the air. One frightened ant turned to another and said in panic, "We'd better get on the ball if we want to stay alive!"

So it is with all of us. There is a time to think, but also a time to do. There is a time to learn, but also a time to act. There is a time to gather information, but also a time to make decisions.

It's been said that knowing something doesn't make a difference. But taking what you know and doing something with it makes all the difference.

If you have been putting off that decision; if you've been procrastinating about beginning that project; or if you've never gotten around to pursuing that dream which never seems to go away, then this is your nudge to get on the ball. It's the only way to really live!

An End To The Anger

Imagine a fine, spring day. A man is driving cheerfully along a picturesque road, which winds through the lazy countryside. Suddenly, from around the next curve, a car barrels toward him in his lane. He brakes hard, and as it swerves past, the woman driver screams at him, "Pig! Pig!"

Furious, he shouts back at her, "Sow! Sow!" Pleased with himself, he drives around the curve and runs smack into a pig.

Anyone can get angry. But as Daniel Goleman in his audio tape *Emotional Intelligence* (St. Martin's Press, Inc., 1995) points out, to be angry with the right person, to the right degree, at the right time, for the right purpose and in the right way is *not* so easy. Which is to say, most of the time we may get angry either with the *wrong* person, or to the *wrong* degree, or at the *wrong* time, or for the *wrong* purpose, or in the *wrong* way. But then, that's the way it is with anger. It just happens!

We can't always "do anger right," so ancient biblical wisdom offers an excellent solution for managing it. It teaches, "Don't let the sun set on your anger."

Of course, problems cannot always be solved by bedtime, and deep-seated anger may take time to heal. But even anger needs an ending time.

Maybe it is time to put an end to anger you have carried far too long. Today?

P.S.

Don't you know that hate is like acid? It eventually eats up the container that holds it.

Acres Of Diamonds

A century ago, Russell Conwell traveled the United States with a speech he called, "Acres of Diamonds." He told of a young man who studied at Yale to become a mining engineer. Upon graduation, "gold fever" struck him and he set off to California to seek his fortune.

Yale had offered him a position as an instructor, which he turned down. He persuaded his mother to sell their Massachusetts farm and accompany him. But the trip was futile as he found no gold and eventually accepted a job in Minnesota working for a mining company – at a lower salary than he would have received at Yale.

More interesting is that the man who bought the family farm from the widowed mother was harvesting potatoes one day. As he slid a heavy bushel through an opening in the stone wall, he noticed a shiny stone. He had it assayed and learned it was native silver. The farm was sitting on a fortune in silver!

Why had the mining engineer, who had undoubtedly passed by that same rock and others like it hundreds of times, not discovered the ore? Could it be that he never dreamed a treasure could be found so easily? Was it because he believed that one must go elsewhere to fulfill a dream?

What we are seeking may be found right where we are! There are certainly times to make life changes, but sometimes we must simply change our thinking. What you seek (happiness, security, fulfillment, challenge) may be at your fingertips, though yet unseen.

There may be hidden potential in your present job, your current relationships or the location in which you live. The answers to your dreams may be found at your fingertips if you only believe it is possible. Before making that big life change, look carefully around. You may be sitting on acres of diamonds!

Live Your Love

Imagine four Army chaplains during an icy storm at sea; four men in uniform holding hands as they gaze over the rail of their sinking vessel. They are watching lifeboats pulling away from their reeling ship, the U.S. transport Dorchester. The story of these chaplains is a remarkable account of love and sacrifice.

The scene takes place February 3, 1943, off the southern tip of Greenland. The winter night covers the ship like a blanket. Most of the 909 aboard ship are asleep below the decks.

Suddenly the Dorchester jerks and shudders. A German torpedo has smashed through her starboard side! In a raging torrent, the sea spurts through the gaping wound. The Dorchester has been dealt a mortal blow. She is sinking.

An order is given to abandon ship. Aboard the dying vessel, men – many of them injured – search frantically for life jackets. Some stand in shock, not knowing how to react to the catastrophe.

Amidst the chaos stand four pillars of strength, four Army chaplains: George L. Fox, Methodist; Alexander Goode, Jewish; Clark V. Poling, Reformed; and John P. Washington, Roman Catholic. They calm the panic-stricken, help the confused search for life jackets and aid the soldiers into the lifeboats swinging out from the tilting deck.

When no more jackets can be found, each chaplain takes off his own and straps it onto a soldier who has none. The lifeboats pull slowly away from the doomed vessel. Only 299 will finally survive this night.

As the Dorchester slides beneath the icy water, some can see the four chaplains, hand in hand, praying to the God of them all. The chaplains' different theological opinions did not seem to matter much on a sinking ship. All that mattered was that, at a time of crisis, they *lived their love*. Yet even for us, every day in lesser ways, I suspect that's all that ever matters.

P.S.

We are always getting ready to live, but never living. ~ *Ralph Waldo Emerson*

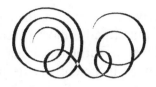

Equip The Children

Should we chain our children to the bedpost until they reach adulthood? Should we shield them from all negative influences until they can make mature decisions?

When Dr. Willis Tate was at Southern Methodist University in Dallas, Texas, he told of a mother who gallantly tried to protect her son. She wrote a long letter to Dr. Tate about her son who was coming to enroll as a freshman. She wanted the president to make sure that the boy had a "good" roommate who would encourage him to go to church and not use bad language. She did not want the roommate to smoke or otherwise negatively influence her son.

But the mother's closing remarks make the letter unforgettable: "The reason all of this is so important is that it is the first time my boy has been away from home, except for the three years he spent in the Marines."

Parents want to protect their children. But perhaps more importantly, most parents want their children to develop sufficient inner resources to protect themselves in potentially destructive situations. They want to equip them to be independent, to make responsible decisions on their own.

Which means that, as their children grow into adulthood, parents must gradually learn to give up thinking that they can protect them and endeavor more to love them. And isn't love really what children of *any* age truly need from their parents?

Look Up

Newscaster Paul Harvey once related a story about a woman from Michigan who vacationed in Florida. She found a secluded spot on the roof of her hotel to soak up a few rays of sunshine, and in order to get a "total" tan, she removed all her clothing. Within a half-hour, the hotel manager was beside her insisting that she cover up. She argued that nobody was in sight. He agreed. Problem was – she was stretched out over the hotel skylight!

It occurs to me that the hotel's problems began because somebody was *looking up*! Which normally is an excellent thing to do. At least in attitude. And what a surprise lay in store that day for those who were looking up!

You see, some folks spend their lives *looking down*. Downcast in spirit, they hang their heads and lead negative and joyless lives.

Others are constantly *looking out.* They live in fear and watch vigilantly for problems, real or imaginary, that threaten their happiness.

Still others seem always to be *looking around.* Forever searching for a better partner, a better job or a better deal, they keep a watchful eye out and seldom experience a lasting commitment.

But a few vibrant folks can usually be found *looking up!* These resilient individuals have learned how to look beyond problems to solutions; beyond discouragement to hope. And quite often, the pay-off is joy.

No matter if your habit is to *look down, look out, look around,* or *look up,* the only important question is, in which direction will you look today?

P.S.

May I never miss a rainbow or a sunset because I am looking down.

You Were Meant For The Skies

This story reminds us how important a healthy self-image really is.

A man found an eagle's egg and put it in a nest of a barnyard hen. The eagle hatched with the brood of chicks and grew up with them. All his life, the eagle did what the barnyard chicks did, thinking he was a barnyard chicken. He scratched the earth for worms and insects. He clucked and cackled. And he thrashed his wings and flew a few feet in the air.

Years passed and the eagle grew very old. One day he saw a magnificent bird above him in the cloudless sky. It glided in graceful majesty among powerful wind currents, with scarcely a beat of its strong, golden wings.

The old eagle looked up in awe. "Who's that?" he asked. "That's the eagle, the king of the birds," said his neighbor. "He belongs to the sky. We belong to the earth – we're chickens." So the eagle lived and died a chicken, for that is what he thought he was. (Author unknown)

You were meant for the skies – not the chicken coop. Who will believe in you if you do not believe in yourself?

Secret To Understanding

It was the late 1940s. Eastern Airline's chair, Captain Eddie Rickenbacker, had a problem. Customers were complaining because the airline was mishandling luggage far too often. When nothing else seemed to work, he decided to take drastic action.

Rickenbacker called a special meeting of the management personnel in Miami. Eastern's management flew to Miami and was told their baggage would be delivered to their hotel rooms. Instead, Rickenbacker had the luggage stored overnight.

It was summer, the weather was hot and humid and the hotel had no air-conditioning. The various managers showed up to the meeting the next morning unshaven, teeth unbrushed and wearing dirty clothes.

There was no sign of the baggage all that day. But that night Rickenbacker had it delivered, at 3:00 a.m., with a great pounding on all the doors.

He opened the next morning's session by saying, "Now you know how the customer feels when you mishandle his luggage." He knew his team would be ineffective until his people empathized with their customers!

The same is true with us. Until we understand another's problem, we will never be effective in business or relationships. And the deepest understanding occurs when we actually sense what the other is feeling. When husbands and wives, parents and children, friends, colleagues, and associates will take time to feel what the other is feeling, something wonderful is likely to happen.

Sounds to me like a chance worth taking!

P.S.

I like to keep a sense of humility about giving advice. After all, there is some truth in the adage that if it's free, it's advice; if you pay for it, it's counseling; and if you can use either one, it's a miracle!

One Minute Can Change A Life

He almost killed somebody, but one minute changed his life. The beautiful story comes from Sherman Rogers' old book, *Foremen: Leaders or Drivers?* In his true-life story, Rogers illustrates the importance of effective relationships.

During his college years, Rogers spent a summer in an Idaho logging camp. When the superintendent had to leave for a few days, he put Rogers in charge.

"What if the men refuse to follow my orders?" Rogers asked. He thought of Tony, an immigrant worker who grumbled and growled all day, giving the other men a hard time.

"Fire them," the superintendent said. Then, as if reading Rogers' mind, he added, "I suppose you think you are going to fire Tony if you get the chance. I'd feel badly about that. I have been logging for 40 years. Tony is the most reliable worker I've ever had. I know he is a grouch and that

159

he hates everybody and everything. But he comes in first and leaves last. There has not been an accident for eight years on the hill where he works."

Rogers took over the next day. He went to Tony and spoke to him. "Tony, do you know I'm in charge here today?" Tony grunted. "I was going to fire you the first time we tangled, but I want you to know I'm not," he told Tony, adding what the superintendent had said.

When he finished, Tony dropped the shovelful of sand he had held and tears streamed down his face. "Why he no tell me dat eight years ago?"

That day Tony worked harder than ever before – and he smiled! He later said to Rogers, "I told Maria you first foreman in deese country who ever say, 'Good work, Tony,' and it make Maria feel like Christmas."

Rogers went back to school after that summer. Twelve years later he met Tony again. He was superintendent for railroad construction for one of the largest logging companies in the West. Rogers asked him how he came to California and happened to have such success.

Tony replied, "If it not be for the one minute you talk to me back in Idaho, I keel somebody someday. One minute, she change my whole life."

Effective managers know the importance of taking a moment to point out what a worker is doing well. But what a difference a minute of affirmation can make in *any* relationship!

One minute. Have you got one minute to thank someone? A minute to tell someone what you sincerely *like* or *appreciate* about her? A minute to elaborate on something he did well? One minute. It can make a difference for a lifetime.

Index

Index, cont.

Quick Order Form

☞ **F**ax Orders: 413-431-3499. Send this form.

☞ **T**elephone Orders: Toll free: 877-344-0989

☞ **W**eb Site Orders: visit
http://www.LifeSupportSystem.com/books

☞ **P**ostal Orders: Life Support System Publishing P.O.
Box 237 Divide, CO 80814 USA

Order these books by Steve Goodier: $12.95
Colorado residents add sales tax: $.39 per book

❑ *One Minute Can Change a Life*   Quantity____
❑ *Riches of the Heart*   Quantity____
❑ *Joy Along the Way*   Quantity____
❑ *Prescription for Peace*   Quantity____
❑ *Touching Moments*   Quantity____

Name _____

Address:_____

_____

E-mail address_____

FREE Shipping and Handling for U.S.A. & Canada
Mexico: $2.00 / book. Other International: $4.00 / book

Would you like FREE gift wrapping?_____

Payment: ___ Check ___ Credit Card:
___Visa ___Master Card ___AMEX

Card #: _____Exp. date: _____

Receive daily inspirational e-mail FREE... visit:
www.LifeSupportSystem.com

Quick Order Form

☞ Fax Orders: 413-431-3499. Send this form.

☞ Telephone Orders: Toll free: 877-344-0989

☞ Web Site Orders: visit
http://www.LifeSupportSystem.com/books

☞ Postal Orders: Life Support System Publishing P.O.
Box 237 Divide, CO 80814 USA

Order these books by Steve Goodier: $12.95
Colorado residents add sales tax: $.39 per book

❑ *One Minute Can Change a Life*   Quantity____
❑ *Riches of the Heart*   Quantity____
❑ *Joy Along the Way*   Quantity____
❑ *Prescription for Peace*   Quantity____
❑ *Touching Moments*   Quantity____

Name _____

Address:_____

_____

E-mail address_____

FREE Shipping and Handling for U.S.A. & Canada
Mexico: $2.00 / book. Other International: $4.00 / book

Would you like FREE gift wrapping?_____

Payment: ___ Check ___ Credit Card:
___Visa ___Master Card ___AMEX

Card #: _____Exp. date: _____

Receive daily inspirational e-mail FREE... visit:
www.LifeSupportSystem.com